Who's in Control?

Decision-making by people with learning difficulties who have high support needs

James Edge

Values Into Action
2001

Copyright © 2001
Values Into Action
London

Written by
James Edge

Published in 2001 by
Values Into Action
Oxford House
Derbyshire Street
London E2 6HG

Tel: 020 7729 5436
Fax: 020 7729 7797
Website: www.viauk.org

Registered Charity Number 1057249
A Company Limited by Guarantee
Registered in England Number 3229730

Distribution
Further copies of 'Who's in Control?' can be obtained from the publisher Values Into
Action

ISBN 0 903945 56 8

This publication includes images from CorelDRAW 9 that are protected by the
copyright laws of the US, Canada, and elsewhere (used under licence) and images
from the Change Picturebank.

Design, production, printing by
ArtZone Co-op Ltd
10 BackChurch Lane
London E1 1LX
tel: 020 7481 9053
email: artzone@and.org.uk

SUPPORTED BY
JR
JOSEPH
ROWNTREE
FOUNDATION

Publishers statement: The Joseph Rowntree Foundation has supported this project
as part of its programme of research and innovative development projects, which it
hopes will be of value to policy makers and practitioners. The facts presented and
views expressed in this report, however, are those of the author and not necessarily
those of the Foundation.

ACKNOWLEDGEMENTS

With thanks to Emma Stone of the Joseph Rowntree Foundation and members of the advisory group, all at Values Into Action, and everyone who has supported the research in some way. Thank you to Sofia Ferreira for the chapter pictures. Special thanks to Carla for all her help and support.

Very special thanks to all the participants in this project. ☺

"The child is taught that he is free,
a democrat, with a free will and a free mind,
lives in a free country, makes his own decisions.
At the same time he is a prisoner of the assumptions
and dogmas of his time, which he does not question,
because he has never been told they exist."

Doris Lessing, *The Golden Notebook*, 1993

"How big is a feeling? Where is the dial that registers in degrees?"

William Golding, *Free Fall*, 1959

Note

The term 'people with learning difficulties' has been used in this report in preference to 'people with learning disabilities', 'an intellectual impairment' or 'mental handicap', because it is the term which people who have to live with the label say they prefer.

In order to preserve confidentiality, all the names and some personal details of the people mentioned in this report have been changed.

Who's in Control?

CONTENTS

1 INTRODUCTION

Over the last 30 years there has been a greater move towards the inclusion and participation of people with learning difficulties in ordinary communities. There has been a move towards independent living and away from traditional institutional approaches of care (Collins, 1996), an increase in individualised funding arrangements (Bewley, 1997), and a renewed interest in decision-making and the law. These developments have shown that people with learning difficulties can be at the centre of decisions about their lives, even if they require substantial support (Canadian Association for Community Living, 1998; Kinsella, 1993; Sanderson et al, 1997; Simons, 1995; Walsh, 1994). Despite this progress many people with learning difficulties who have high support needs are frequently prevented from having choice or control over even basic decisions in their lives (Bewley, 1998; Wertheimer, 2000; Collins, 1996; Ryan and Holman, 1998). This may be done directly (for example, by taking away people's money so they cannot choose how it is spent), or indirectly (for example, by failing to communicate effectively with people with learning difficulties so their preferences are not known).

Supporting people to make decisions

People who do not use speech or sign or do not respond clearly to questions nevertheless express their likes and dislikes through sound, behaviour and expressions. In order to respect everyone's right to self-determination, how people express their preferences must be recognised and used as starting point to making decisions. With the appropriate support and opportunities people who have high support needs can be in control of complex decisions, such as where to live, who to live with or what to do during the day.

Relationships and communication are at the heart of supporting people to make decisions. Given appropriate time and contact, it is possible to get to know someone's usual way of communicating. Those in close contact with the individual may well have the best understanding of their communication.

Supporting people make choices mirrors the way everyone makes decisions. If a person is thinking about moving house, they will ask friends and family what they think, buy newspapers and magazines to see what is available, and visit a few properties. They may find out about Housing Associations, part buy schemes or council housing. When making complex decisions people will look for support and help from a wide range of sources. Sometimes, decisions are based on little more than a feeling or notion, a lot is left to chance or there is an element of risk. It is impossible to consider and objectively weigh all possible outcomes of personal decisions, and it is not always possible to know why one choice is better than another. People with learning difficulties should not be expected to make perfect decisions or make them better than anyone else.

Decisions that are made on someone else's behalf without their involvement may, in some cases, be made unlawfully and, in all cases, are made against the principles of good practice. In order to protect the right of people to make their own decisions and to ensure that decisions presented reflect the choices of the individual concerned it is necessary to provide evidence that demonstrates how the decision was made. Such evidence should demonstrate the individual was in control of the final decision, even if they needed a great deal of support to make a choice or put their choice into effect.

More formal evidence will be needed for a decision with serious consequences. How information is gathered and recorded is important in establishing who is in control. Keeping accurate and up-to-date records is essential for service providers. If challenged, people involved such as local authority staff, should demonstrate that decisions were made lawfully or without maladministration. The research upon which this book is based aimed to identify practical ways in which it can be demonstrated that someone with learning difficulties is in control of decisions.

Context: policy and legislation

Legislation and guidance around decision-making have been notable by their absence. However, change to the law is underway in England and Wales. Scotland has already introduced legislation (Adults with Incapacity Scotland Act 2000), which is being implemented during 2001. Chapter 4 looks at these developments across the UK, and questions how far they go in protecting people's right to choice and control.

Community Care

Involvement and participation are key elements in legislation. The NHS and Community Care Act 1990 (NHSCC Act) makes several references about the need to "inform, consult and involve people who use services".

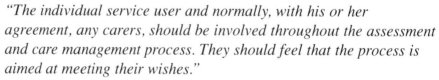

"The individual service user and normally, with his or her agreement, any carers, should be involved throughout the assessment and care management process. They should feel that the process is aimed at meeting their wishes."

Department of Health 1990, p25

However, this research suggests that people who have learning difficulties generally have little or no say in services they receive. While choice is scattered about community care guidance, it is absent from legislation (Department of Health, 1990). Local authorities, not the individuals themselves, make final decisions about people's needs and service provision.

One of the disadvantages of the NHSCC Act is that it puts duties on local authorities to provide services, rather than giving rights to individuals to receive them. It is also only relevant where someone is in the care management system. However, services that are tailored to individual needs give people who use services more choice and control. Policy guidance mentions the exercising of 'genuine choice' and the participation in the assessment process of people who use or might use services. Guidance also recognises the inequality of relationships between people who provide services and those who use them – "the present imbalance can be corrected by sharing information more openly and by encouraging users and carers ... to take a full part in decision-making" (Department of Health, 1990).

Access to information about services is fundamental to the process of making choices and decisions, and services have a duty to provide this information in a variety of formats. Accessible information should be available "to enable users and carers to exercise genuine choice and participation in the assessment of their care needs and in the making of arrangements for meeting those needs" (Department of Health 1990, p26). Community Care Plans must address how information will be made available to potential users of services, how consumer choice will be managed and what it will involve (Department of Health, 1990)

Direct payments

Local Authorities now have the power to give money directly to disabled people instead of providing a service. The Community Care (Direct Payments) Act 1996 allows people to receive money to pay for their own support, following an assessment of their needs. For example, if someone is unhappy at the local day centre, then they could use a direct payment to purchase support to enable them go to the local college, find a job or engage in a whole range of activities to meet these assessed needs, when, where and how they want. Clearly, direct payments enable people with learning difficulties to really control their own lives by controlling how, when and where they receive their support, and from whom (Holman & Bewley, 1999; Ryan & Holman 1998; Bewley, 1997; Holman, 1995).

Human rights

The Human Rights Act 1998 (HRA) came into force in October 2000. It means that the rights and protection of the European Convention of Human Rights have now been implemented into UK legislation. It has huge potential in supporting legal claims by people with learning difficulties and ensuring their human rights are not breached.

The main aim of the HRA is to bring about a culture shift in organisations, such as local authorities. Public authorities should ask themselves whether the policies, practices, and decisions they make need to be revised in order not to infringe someone's human rights. The relevant articles of the HRA are outlined in the Appendix.

About this book

Despite these developments, many barriers exist that prevent people with high support needs from making choices and influencing decisions. Some will concern the individual, such as communication or motivation. Many others will concern the environment around the individual, such as attitudes and assumptions about an individual's ability, access to information, or lack of opportunities to make choices.

This book will look at complex decisions, such as where people live, with whom, who provides support, how money is spent or what to do during the day. The term high support needs is used to indicate when someone needs significant support to live their daily lives.

Chapter 2 looks at decision-making in practice, and highlights some of the common issues when making decisions with people who have high support needs.

Demonstrating that someone is in control of decisions will involve building up a picture of how a decision was reached. Chapter 3 looks at practical ways in which people with learning difficulties can influence the decision-making process. Ways to record this information and presenting evidence in formal situations are discussed.

The legal situation around making decisions, and how the law does not protect the rights of everyone to make their own decisions is discussed in chapter 4.

The conclusions and key recommendations from each of the sections are drawn together in chapter 5.

Further information about the research on which this book is based, and relevant legislation and case law affecting decision-making can be found in the Appendices. A glossary of words, a list of contacts and references can also be found in the Appendices.

The Project

The research was carried out across four sites in England and Scotland between August 1999 and January 2001. The aims of the research were to find practical ways in which it can be demonstrated that someone with learning difficulties and high support needs is in control of decisions and how this evidence fits into the legal context around decision-making. Participants were selected to represent a cross section of geographical location, types of living and support arrangements, cultural and other factors. Semi-structured interviews and observations were carried out with 15 participants living in nine homes (Social Services & independent provider residential homes, independent living environments, and family homes) and those who support them. Additional information was gained through documentation on policies and procedures, and visits to other key organisations. A fuller description of the methodology can be found in Appendix A.

2 DECISION-MAKING IN PRACTICE

This chapter looks at how decisions are made in practice by and with people with learning difficulties. It begins by defining some of the terms used in this report, and describes how decisions are categorised in a legal context. It will then look at the experiences of the participants and current practice around making decisions. Particular focus will be made on some of the challenges involved in providing support and the barriers people with learning difficulties face when making choices and decisions.

Decisions, choice and control

The words decision, choice and control are commonly used when talking about making decisions. These words need to be defined before they can be discussed in more detail.

Choice is defined as the option of indicating 'yes' or 'no' to something, or selecting between a number of options. Choice is about being recognised and valued as an individual human being. We make choices in what we eat, how we dress, where we live, with whom, and where we work. Personal choice is about the way we live our lives the way we want. It defines individual identity; how we would like to see ourselves, and how we would like others to see us.

Decisions mean that final choices have been made. A decision is reached at the end of the process of choosing. Decision-making is the process by which people make choices or express their preferences, leading to action. In a legal context, decisions have been divided into three main areas, financial, welfare and health. Each of these areas has different legal and practice implications.

Welfare   Decisions will include day-to-day decisions, such as what to eat, where to live, and what to do during the day.

Financial   Decisions will include managing finances, bank accounts, collecting Social Security benefits and spending money.

Health   Decisions will include consenting to medical treatment, health screening and routine check-ups, and medication.

While these categories may be useful for legal purposes, decisions made in real life do not fit into these discrete boxes. Decisions can impact on some or all of these areas, and the approach to supporting people make these decisions will be the same.

Control is about having self-determination. It is about people having autonomy and power over their own lives and what happens to them, regardless of how much support they need to put their choices into action. Control is about independence but independence does not mean people have to live alone or do everything for themselves. Independence is about people being able to direct or 'determine' their own lives, rather than being constrained by the systems and structures of service organisations.

For example, direct payments give someone control over their support by giving them control over the money needed to buy their support. The issue is not whether or not someone needs help to do their weekly household shopping, for instance, but whether they are in charge of when and how they shop, what they buy, and what the support worker does to help. Someone who needs continual intensive support and who has limited understanding of the complexities of decision-making can still control their life if their choices and preferences directly influence decisions.

Preference is another word for choice or wish. Some people with high support needs are not able to make clear, informed decisions about complex matters. Nevertheless, everyone expresses preferences - likes, dislikes, happiness, comfort, pleasure and so on. These preferences are absolutely central to decision-making. They are the core building blocks of a proactive decision-making process that demonstrates that an individual is determining their own life.

What happens in practice?

People who took part in the study had different experiences around making decisions. Paul is supported to live independently, and so now he has many new choices, and after her first long-term relationship Beverley has become more assertive and confident about making her own decisions. Some services were beginning to listen to what people were indicating; Jack's needs were not being met at the day-centre and he had started a forest skills course through his local college. Other participants had less choice and control over decisions; Martin was being moved to a new house because the neighbours had complained about sounds he made in the garden, and Ralph attends the local day-centre chosen by a social worker without his involvement.

Jack's story below illustrates the common experiences of people who have high support needs, who are frequently not given the opportunity or support to make decisions or influence how they are made.

Four years ago, Jack lived in a long stay hospital. When the hospital closed, Jack was moved to a residential home with five other people. Since then he has attended a local day centre. At the day centre Jack takes part in a number of different activities that the centre provides. Jack did not have any say in where he was moved, with whom he lived or who supports him. The day centre he attends was chosen by his social worker.

DECISION-MAKING IN PRACTICE

However, people who have learning difficulties and high support needs can make and be involved in decisions about their lives. Everyone can communicate their likes, dislikes and preferences in some way.

Over one year, Jack had been indicating through his behaviour that he was unsatisfied with the services he received. He would be uninterested in taking part in activities at the day-centre and staff had noticed that he was unhappy when he came back from the day centre. In response, staff tried out new activities with Jack so he could find out what else was available. They found that he was happy doing activities that were not offered at the day centre. They looked at other things they knew about him in order to guide these activities, such as the fact that he liked being around other people and being outdoors.

There are also barriers created by the way in which service organisations are funded, staffed and run. Organisations favour routine, regularity and the status quo. Responding to truly individual choices and needs is difficult for a bureaucracy. Systems and structures can stifle staff initiative and imagination or create a climate of fear and over-protection around any sort of 'risky' change. These attitudes are also engrained in wider social structures. People with higher support needs may find themselves labeled as 'mentally incapable' of making their own decisions and subject to decisions made 'in their best interests' by others, often without guidance, monitoring or the opportunity to effectively challenge those substitute decisions.

Factors that affect personal decision-making

Choices can be very difficult to make, particularly when decisions are complex and have important consequences. Decision-making can be stressful, because of the emotions felt when there are conflicting options, when contradictory advice is given, or when the choice affects other people. People who are not able to understand complex information and those who find it difficult to communicate their choices often find themselves left out of decisions made about their lives. It may require more time or a change in how supporters interact with people but everyone can be enabled to be at the heart of decision-making about their lives.

How to make choices and take control of our lives is something we all learn; none of us is born able to make complex decisions. Institutionalisation and over-protection deny people the opportunity to grow in their decision-making confidence and ability. People may have had few opportunities to make choices, or those they do make are consistently ignored. People's motivation to make decisions may not be very high; in effect people learn that they have no control over decisions (Seligman, 1953). Some participants in the research had little or no say in many decisions in their lives. Their choices in the past have been consistently ignored or not acted upon and so they are less likely to believe they can influence other decisions.

For example, Daniel would like to change his support worker, as they do not get on very well. Daniel's social worker asked him whether he would like to extend the contract of his supporter, but did not take into account how difficult this decision could be. Now that the support worker's contract has been renewed, it will be hard for Daniel to change to someone else. Daniel said that he did not have enough time to make the decision, or the support he wanted.

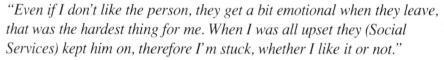

"Even if I don't like the person, they get a bit emotional when they leave, that was the hardest thing for me. When I was all upset they (Social Services) kept him on, therefore I'm stuck, whether I like it or not."

Daniel

Throughout the research sites a number of factors were identified that might affect someone's ability to influence decisions:

- how someone communicates;
- the extent to which someone understands the information or what is expected of them;
- the extent to which someone can remember the information;
- different personal values and attitudes;
- a possible tendency to indicate 'yes' to questions asked);
- lack of motivation or experience to make choices.

Other factors are concerned with the environment around the individual. Limited time, lack of resources, restricted finances, differing values between supporters, and lack of support or staff shortages were common across all of the research sites. These factors reduce someone's choices and opportunities, and their chance to control their own life. However, these are not insurmountable barriers or an inevitable part of how services work. There are practical ways in which staff and supporters can shift how they work as individuals and as teams with people with high support needs. There are also ways in which service organisations need to change to effectively enable staff to empower the people with learning difficulties that they work with in decision-making about their lives.

Summary of challenges and barriers to people having choice and control

- How much time is available to make choices.
- How the information is presented.
- Mismatched power relationship between services and people who use them.
- The nature of relationships with supporters.
- Limited opportunities.
- Staff needing support and training.
- People 'not allowed' to make mistakes.
- Lack of time, resources and staff shortages.
- Families making the decisions without proper information or support.
- Undiagnosed sight and hearing impairments.
- People being labeled as 'challenging' and having their views dismissed as a result.
- Attitudes that 'professionals know best'.

- Limiting and possibly incorrect attitudes and assumptions about someone's abilities.
- Lack of awareness for cultural differences.
- Lack of advocacy, peer support or a 'champion'.
- Limitations of social security benefits system and control of money.

Power relationships in decision-making

There is an unequal balance of power between services and those who use them (Bewley, 1998; Perkins and Repper, 1998). Services can limit an individual's choice, and hence her or his control over decisions (Gilbert, 1995). People have decisions made for them on the basis of someone's opinion or as a result of changes to services or resources. One participant, Martin, is being moved to a new house because the neighbours have complained about noises he makes in the garden. After the neighbours complained to the head of the service that supported him it was decided that he should move without fully investigating the claim. The presence of an easy to access complaints procedure is imperative to enable people to challenge such decisions.

Rules that are introduced by services, perhaps to regulate how resources are used, can also restrict people's freedom. One participant, Daniel, lived in a residential home that had one minibus for all of the residents. If he wanted to go out shopping or to the cinema he would have to give a week's notice. Many people find that their days are structured according to the needs of the service and its staff, rather than their own needs and wants. Direct payments have been one way by which some people with learning difficulties have broken out of this situation. However, very few people with learning difficulties have been supported to access direct payments. Some restrictions have been caused by a disproportionate panic by service organisations around the issue of control. Those people with higher support needs who are accessing direct payments prove that, with the right support, people can be enabled to be in control of their direct payments (Henderson and Bewley, 2000).

The imbalance of power between those who use services and those who provide them can be seen clearly in the issue of 'risk'. A number of people who worked within services found that enabling people to make decisions and take risks within the service system was difficult and that services were unwilling to hand power over to people who use the service.

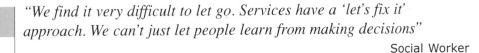

"We find it very difficult to let go. Services have a 'let's fix it' approach. We can't just let people learn from making decisions"

Social Worker

Risk is part of life: nobody grows as a human being without the chance to try new things and take risks. Many people with learning difficulties find their right to take the sort of risks that others take for granted severely restricted. If the individual has the legal right to make their own choice, this restriction may even be illegal (see chapter 4).

Where decisions are made

People who have high support needs and live within service provision frequently have little or no control over their lives on any more than a superficial level (Collins,1996; Bewley, 1997). There can be set ways of doing things or patterns of services that are difficult to break out of. These can sometimes be based on assumptions or attitudes about what should happen to people with learning difficulties, rather than looking beyond service options. For example, one of the participants was moving out from a residential home, only to be put on a waiting list for another group living arrangement, without consideration of whether he might want to live alone or with others. Services that make these decisions without finding out what someone's wishes and preferences are and then trying to act on what they find out, will be ignoring the principles of choice, participation and involvement. They may also be overriding people's legal right to make decisions. For a fuller discussion about the legal situation around decision-making see chapter 4.

Someone's support arrangements may be reviewed if their service is costing more than has been contractually agreed, perhaps because the service is no longer meeting their needs, or the service is unable to cope. For example, if someone refuses to take part in activities, or they start to injure themselves or others, these behaviours will be labeled 'challenging behaviours', rather than recognising that they might be trying to communicate something.

One social worker who participated in the research outlined the possible response if someone starts to 'challenge' a day service.

Service requests increased funding to meet needs.

Services asked to find the requirements from within existing funds due to budget pressures.

Individual excluded from service as it is deemed to no longer meet their needs

Carers pick up additional burden until they can no longer cope.

Individual placed in residential unit.

Family relationships are often damaged.

Such a pattern will probably not be the most appropriate for the individual or their family. It does not take into account possible reasons for the change in behaviour and what it might be communicating. The wishes and preferences of the individual are therefore lost and decisions are made without her or his involvement. The social worker in this example was able to develop a service that responded to the needs of the two individuals involved, Jane and David. He recognised that their behaviours were expressions of dislike about the day centre and thus the basis of their choice not to attend. He then looked for creative ways to fund alternative day services. The case study of Jane and David is described in more detail later in chapter 3.

When decisions are made

For people who use services, some major life decisions are made as part of the individual planning process. However, individual planning may not include the person or their supporters effectively or, indeed, at all. The experience of many participants was that major decisions were initiated by staff, often in reaction to specific situations. These decisions did not necessarily reflect the wishes of the individual.

The following example of Paul's experiences around decision-making, show that supporting people to make choices is an ongoing process. Choices and preferences can then inform decision-making at key stages, such as at review meetings. Records then need to show how Paul's choices have influenced decisions that have been made.

> *Paul is in his late 20's. He used to live in a group home, but was very keen to get a place of his own. He was also nervous about moving out and living by himself. With help from support staff from an independent support agency he has now lived in a rented house for the last 18 months. Staff spent time with Paul looking at all the different options available and visiting different flats and houses. As choices and decisions arose along the way, staff would help Paul look at the choices available and their implications.*

People who use services should have some form of individual plan that describes their needs and how they are being met. In order for people to have control over all aspects of their lives, these plans need to take into account the preferences of the individual with regard to both assessed needs and other choices and decisions.

A number of planning tools exist that help find out what someone wants and what supporters need to do to make these choices happen. These tools are grouped under the heading 'person centred planning' (Sanderson et al, 1997). One person-centred tool is called Essential Lifestyle Planning (ELP). ELPs provide a framework for staff to find out what someone wants and how to record this information. Four research participants had ELPs. If these plans are seen as an ongoing process then it reflects how people change their minds, try out new things and develop new skills.

> *Paul had an ELP that listed things such as what he liked doing, when and with whom, what he disliked and how he communicated. It offered a way in which Paul's ambitions and needs were recorded, planned for and discussed. Sections of his plan included 'non-negotiable' items, such as 'I want to visit my family at every weekend'. Other*

sections list things he would like to happen in the future, such as 'I would like to have my kitchen decorated' or 'I would like to get a job'. Paul changed his mind and wanted to try out new activities quite often, so it was important that Paul and all the staff were involved in keeping the records up to date. Every few months the ELP would be reviewed. A communication book used by staff helped everyone remember what had happened since the last meeting. The service manager provided on-going training and helped looked for ways staff and the agency could help Paul achieve what he wanted.

The only way in which such planning tools work is if everyone is committed to supporting the individual live the way they want to. There can be a tendency for staff and organisations to think of the people who use the service as a group of people with similar needs. This highlights the importance of person-centred approaches to planning and questioning assumptions about what services think someone's needs are.

Lucy and Michelle have lived together for about eight years. Many of their support staff have known them for many years. Lucy and Michelle were moved in together because they have similar support needs; both of them have learning difficulties and use a wheelchair. Since carrying out Essential Lifestyle Plans, staff have really focused on what each of the women is communicating through her behaviour. This information has altered the service's perception that they are similar people who should live together to Lucy and Michelle being seen as individuals with very different personalities and aspirations.

Summary

Organisations need to address how people who use their services are enabled to make decisions and given the opportunities to do so. People who do not use verbal communication can lose their right to make decisions because the ways in which they communicate their preferences are not recognised or not used to influence decisions. People involved can face many challenges in demonstrating that decisions presented are truly those of the individual. The following chapter looks at practical ways in which an individual can be involved and supported to make decisions, put them into practice, and hence be in control of their lives.

- All people have a right to make their own choices about their own lives.
- People can be prevented from having choice and control in their lives for a variety of reasons.
- Everyone can communicate their preferences and choices in some way.
- With the right support everyone can control decisions that are made.

3 EVIDENCE OF CONTROL

> *"None of these organisations think I understand. They don't understand!*
> *They say who you should work with and you have to stick with it through thick and thin"*
>
> Daniel, talking about services

This chapter describes ways in which organisations and supporters can ensure that people with learning difficulties are in control of decisions. A number of case studies are presented to illustrate how people can be control of decision-making. Being clear about how a particular decision was reached is crucial if a decision is challenged.

As noted in chapter 2, being in control of a decision does not necessarily mean that someone has to understand all the complex details involved or that they have to make the decision unaided or that they have to be able to put their choice into effect. This report argues that enabling someone to be in control of their life means enabling them and their expressions of preference and choice to be at the heart of decision-making. From this perspective, no decisions would be made or enacted without clear evidence that this is what the individual wants. Such evidence is built from an effective, recorded process of decision-making by the individual and their supporters.

Demonstrating that someone is in control of a decision involves building up a picture of what their choices are, what support is available and evaluating the outcome of the decision. If it is not clear what the individual wants, then it is even more important that an effective collective process of decision-making has been undertaken. Being clear about how a particular decision is reached is crucial if a decision is challenged.

The more that services are arranged to support people's preferences and respect their rights, the more likely it is that the person will be in control. Across the research sites people had adopted different ways of checking whether decisions made reflect what someone actually wanted. This chapter draws together these different approaches in which someone can be shown to be in control of a decision.

The following sections are organised into the main questions that should be asked when a decision has been reached or when challenging decisions that have already been made.

- What support is available?
- How are choices recognised?

- What are the options?
- Have the decisions been made easier?
- What are the outcomes?
- How have decisions been documented?

Approaching all decisions with these questions in mind will enable people to have control over decisions that are made.

What support is available?

Many people might be involved in the decision-making process, including family members, friends, advocates, staff, doctors, psychologists, speech therapists, a social worker and care manager. Each of these people may have different ideas about what the 'right' decision should be. In demonstrating who is in control of a decision it will therefore be important to establish who is involved in the process, clarify what their roles are and be open about the possible differences in people's agendas.

Nina is in her mid thirties and lives in a residential home with four other people. While at a disco Nina recognised a man called Gareth, whom she used to know. They stayed in touch and their friendship developed. Gareth visited Nina once or twice a week at her home. Nina indicates 'yes' and 'no' by smiling. Because she does not use verbal communication, staff looked for other signs that she wanted the relationship to continue. She was incredibly happy when Gareth visited. On one occasion when Gareth went away on holiday she cried, which staff had never known her to do in the past. Staff would ask her questions after each visit to check with Nina that she still wanted the relationship to continue.

Throughout this time Nina's grandmother was unhappy with the relationship and did not approve of the relationship being supported, and did not want the couple to continue seeing each other. In this situation it was important for the staff to remember that the decision is Nina's alone. The staff were satisfied that Nina wanted the relationship to continue.

After three years into the relationship, Gareth proposed to Nina. The staff felt unsure whether she could consent to marriage and so called in the Community Learning Disability Team (CLDT). The CLDT found that, as Nina was inconsistent in her responses, that staff should not support her to get married.

Whilst it is important to check what someone wants by involving others, it is also important that people do not lose their right to make decisions because professionals are anxious about getting involved in what they see as contentious issues.

This example illustrates a number of issues. First, that people will have different ideas about what is 'best' for the individual and sometimes these ideas clash. It is important to remember the legal situation that, if someone has the capacity to make a decision for him/herself, then they have the right to do so. This legal context applies to all of us, regardless of the labels applied by medical or social service organisations.

However, the example also demonstrates the difficulties that can result for people when formal assessments of capacity are undertaken. As is argued in the next Chapter, such assessments may be inaccurate but they serve to label an individual and restrict their legal rights. Nina's right to marry was taken away when the CLDT assessed her as incapable of making the decision for herself. Although in this case Nina and Gareth later stopped seeing each other and, through the experience, Nina did gain much more confidence about making decisions and standing up for what she wanted, staff should approach the formal assessment of capacity with a great deal of caution. The first step should always be to enhance someone's ability to make a choice for him/herself, to promote their legal right to make decisions and to support them to do so.

Independent advocacy

The role of an independent or citizen advocate is often noted as very important to supporting individuals and protecting their rights (Williams, 1998; Wertheimer, 1998). However, this is limited by the fact that very few people have access to independent advocacy and citizen advocates have no right in law to act as someone's representative.

Advocates may take on a number of roles, such as speaking up for the individual, providing information, finding out what options are available, and protecting the rights of the individual they support. The involvement of an independent voice in the decision-making process may well indicate that the wishes and choices of the individual concerned are being listened to and acted on.

One of the participants, Daniel, had support from a local advocacy scheme. In the past he found making decisions difficult without independent support. Daniel was faced with a decision about whether his support worker's contract should be renewed. He did not have an advocate to help him make this decision. When asked if having an advocate with him would have helped, he replied,

"Yes, because they would say 'hang on a minute what do you think they have done for you in the past'. I would have thought to myself, hang on a minute that person's right and I would have let him go. But instead of that, I was on my own, I didn't have no one to help me. It was either yes or no."

People may not have access to an advocate because there is no legal requirement on services that they should be enabled to have an independent advocate or because there are not always enough volunteer advocates available (Edge and Presley, 1998). Some organisations did recognise the importance of advocacy in their operational policy. One such policy stated, "for people who find it difficult to advocate on their own behalf it is hoped that a suitable person will be found who will be able to act as the resident's advocate". However, good intentions are often not sufficient.

Some staff felt that they advocated on behalf of the people they support but it is important to recognise that this is not the same as independent advocacy, as staff may experience a conflict of interest between the views of the individual and the service. Some staff positively welcome the views of others from outside the service, to make sure that they are actually responding to the wishes of the individual, but others find this threatening.

Not all services involved in this research involved advocates in their work and some felt that it was their decision as to whether someone could have one. Legally, it is up to the individual to decide whether to have an advocate or not and, of course, this often means that those who cannot clearly ask for an independent advocate are denied the opportunity of having one. It is interesting to note that restricting someone's access to advocacy groups may be in breach of the Human Rights Acts 1998 (the relevant sections of the Human Rights Act 1998 are listed in the appendix).

Daniel, quoted in the example above, also received support from other people with learning difficulties who lived in the same area. The importance of contacting other people with learning difficulties or organisations of disabled people had often been overlooked in the research sites as a valuable source of advice, information and peer support.

How are choices recognised?

Recognising how someone communicates and assessing how others communicate with them is fundamental if an individual is to be in control of decision-making. Support workers involved across the research sites said that communication was one of the biggest challenges they faced in finding out what people wanted. Some support staff initially said that the individuals they support could only choose between things like what to eat or what to wear. However, they would go on to say that they also know if someone likes being with others, whether they want to go outside, who their friends are, or whether they are unwell. This reflects a general finding that while people are communicating choices all the time, the choices are often not used as a starting point for making more complex decisions. Everyone can communicate choices in some way. It is the responsibility of supporters to recognise how someone may be communicating these and building them into the decision-making process.

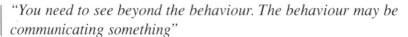

"You need to see beyond the behaviour. The behaviour may be communicating something"

Registered Home Manager

The signs and behaviours that supporters look for may be subtle and or not even deliberate choices, but they can be real indications of what someone wants. Finding out the answers may not be easy and may take time. Staff considered how often the behaviour happened, what was the context, was it aimed at someone or something in particular and what was the intensity of the behaviour. Supporters sometimes had different interpretations about what someone was communicating and so it was necessary to check with each other. These preferences and choices were then used to influence decisions that followed.

> *Beverley is in her late 30's and lives in a residential home. Quite suddenly she started to not want to get up in the mornings. Staff had different ideas about why she wanted to stay in bed. They listed as many possibilities, such as being tired through lack of sleep, not liking breakfast, not wanting to go to the day centre, and so on. They spent several months testing out each of these ideas by observing her behaviour at different times during the morning, and checking out other factors in the environment around her. They asked staff at the day centre whether they had noticed any changes in the mornings. When they spoke to the minibus bus driver that took her to the day centre he mentioned that she would try and reach out towards her friend. They discovered that she liked someone on the day centre minibus, who she was unable to sit next to. This led onto staff supporting Beverley and her friend to see more of each other outside of the day centre.*

The extent to which these choices are acted upon can depend on whether they are recognised in the first place and whether support staff or carers believe something can be done. Organisations that looked creatively at ways to find out what people want, could therefore provide services that responded much better to individual need. One manager of a residential home, who has known one of the participants for a number of years, comments,

> *"Its only over the last four months that we have really started listening to what Michelle is saying."*
>
> Manager of Residential home

People who do not use verbal communication may not be making decisions in a traditional way, but they will be communicating their preferences, likes, dislikes, in many other ways. Beverley, mentioned above, does not use verbal communication and can go for several weeks without responding to other people around her. At other times she will scream very loudly, sing, or quietly whisper to herself and others around her.

Beverley uses a variety of ways to communicate with others:

Sounds, noises	*Flickering eyes*
Physical tension	*Passiveness, lack of interest*
Natural gestures, eye pointing	*Mimicking*
Uneasiness	*Using objects*
Sadness, anger, aggressiveness	*Awareness, reactions*
Restlessness	*Screaming, shouting*
Gestures	*Joy, happiness, laughing, smiling*

Beverley screams loudly in a variety of situations. It was unclear to staff why Beverley was screaming and staff had their own interpretations. Without recognising that her screaming could have been communicating something Beverley would have limited control over her environment. At a staff meeting they discussed possible reasons, and looked at when and where Beverley made these sounds. The staff used a table like the one below to record how and the context in which Beverley screamed. Other people who knew her well were asked to record their interpretations and observations with the involvement of Beverley.

When this is happening	Beverly does this	We think it means	We should do this
Sitting at the breakfast table	Looks upset and screams loudly	I want to eat alone	Have breakfast at a different time

When they looked at the context in which Beverley screamed they found that she would use the same behaviour to send a variety of messages, such as wanting to be alone, wanting some attention, or she was unhappy about something. There are times when the interpretation of someone's communication is not straightforward. Staff approached this challenge by acting collectively. They responded in a consistent way to the screams depending on the context at the time. They checked out their interpretations by looking for other signs that they had got it right. They also shared and discussed their approach and what they found within the team. Out of this they began to see patterns in Beverley's behaviour. This approach has enabled Beverley to have more control over everyday choices and has given the staff insights into how she communicates that will be useful for more complex decision-making in the future.

What are the options?

What options are available for people to choose from will be an important indicator that someone has control over decisions. The more options that are available the more likely it is that someone has selected the one they want. People with learning difficulties are often denied the opportunities to take part in activities beyond those offered by services. Instead, the 'options' for what happens during the day may be restricted to local day centres. Looking at the person's wishes, dreams and aspirations and developing services or activities around these preferences are more likely to reflect individual need.

Sometimes choices and options are restricted because of assumptions about how people with high support needs can or should live. People with learning difficulties should have opportunities to access the same community facilities as everyone else. Many people involved in the study attended services that provided a limited number of activities to do during the day, with little or no choice in which ones they took part in. This highlights the need to look beyond traditional services to the wide range of options available in the wider community. Some participants were prevented from accessing community facilities because of discrimination, such as impractical access or lack of support. Staff in residential homes could challenge service providers to make the appropriate changes on behalf of those they support, using the Disability Discrimination Act 1995 or complaints procedures if necessary.

Have the decisions been made easier?

Some people involved in the research had been able to make complex decisions because the choices involved had been made easier. There a number of ways in which these decisions can be made easier. These must be made explicit when decisions are being made in order to demonstrate that someone has influenced how they are made. Despite the importance of people's involvement in decision-making some services had not considered how people could be effectively involved.

It can be useful to break complex decisions down into smaller more manageable chunks. If the choices have been made easier for a person to make then this is an indicator that someone is being supported to be in control of decisions. Asking smaller questions in a series of stages will help answer the larger question. This is especially useful when there is uncertainty about what someone's choices are, or there are inconsistencies in the choices someone is making.

When moving house, for example, there are a range of factors that will influence how decisions are made. An individual does not need to understand many of the concepts involved in moving house to influence the decision.

Ian communicates in a number of non-verbal ways. Staff are building up a picture of his likes and dislikes and trying out new activities. The kinds of questions they are asking will create a picture of whether Ian wants to move house, and if so, to where. The kinds of questions they asked him, and others who know him well, included:
- did he like living with others?
- what facilities did he like in his current house e.g. being in the kitchen, garden, and so on?
- did he use local facilities, such as the swimming pool, college or park?
- did he want to be near his family or friends?

These kinds of questions may not be asked when making decisions with someone and yet they build a picture of what someone wants. Decisions that are made in someone's 'best interests' should take these kind of questions into account (for a fuller discussion of 'best interests' decision-making see chapter 4).

Access to basic health checks

Some participants had not had an eye or hearing test for a number of years. Having access to regular check-ups can be very important when being able to hear questions or see what is happening. One research participant always had very dirty glasses, which made it difficult for him to see what was going on. Most people are asked verbally what their choices are. This can make it particularly difficult for people who have hearing impairments to make choices, when they may only be hearing part of what is being asked.

Being aware of other possible undiagnosed conditions, such as headaches or being depressed, can also be important when looking at what factors may affect an individual's choices and what they are communicating. These factors should be considered when maximising someone's involvement in decisions.

A number of staff expressed concerns over prescribed medication that had negative side effects, such as drowsiness. For example, two participants who had moved from long-stay hospital had been taken off medication that had not been reviewed for a number of years.

One participant had a generally high level of anxiety that impacted upon his ability to make decisions in his life. His GP had prescribed drugs, commonly given to people who have Asperger's syndrome, which were making him drowsy and not reducing his anxiety. With the help of staff, and by making contact with a support group, he has tried a new medication that he says makes him less anxious without the side effects of previous drugs. This has helped him feel more able to make decisions for himself.

Making information accessible

How information is presented to people will be useful when demonstrating that someone has been effectively involved in a decision. Making information accessible will include making written information easier to understand, but also includes how someone receives the information:

- is the information given by people the person trusts?
- can the person physically access the information?
- trying things out may be one of the ways someone can find out about something;
- who finds out what information is available?

How much information someone needs to understand will depend on the decision in question. Providing information in ways that are accessible to the individual will enable more effective involvement in decisions.

Using a variety of techniques to get the message across can aid communication, such as videos, tapes, group work, games, pictures and talking. Some services provide training in communication skills to staff. One organisation learnt about how videos and tapes can be useful for recording how people communicate with each other, but failed to follow this up with providing the resources necessary. Other services had adopted a number of ways to communicate with people who do not use verbal communication. The staff considered whether someone had sensory impairments. Objects of reference were also adapted accordingly, by using all the senses - touch, sight, hearing, taste and smell.

Ralph carried a communication book around with him that explained how he communicates, and contained pictures and photographs to help him communicate. He can point at the large wipe-clean pictures to indicate he would like something, or pick out photos of friends, family and staff.

This book was reviewed regularly by his key-worker, with input from other staff members. People he met often, such as his music teacher and people at the day centre, would include relevant pictures. Ralph had a busy social life and so it was very useful for when he met new people.

Staff also used objects of reference, where objects associated with a particular activity are used to indicate what is happening or what is being talked about. For example, they held up a towel when they asked Ralph if he wanted to go swimming.

Ralph also attends a day centre. The manager wanted to find out whether people were satisfied with the service they received and then feed this information into service development planning. The manager wrote a questionnaire to send out to all the people attending the centre. Although the questionnaire included easy words, large print and pictures, it was inaccessible to many people using the service. Other imaginative and direct ways of gathering views and experiences needed to be used to ensure that everyone was included. In fact, the questionnaire more actually reflected the views of the parents and staff who filled it in. Despite the best of intentions, many people are similarly excluded from decisions affecting their lives.

Opportunities for making choices

The following example illustrates how people can have the opportunity to make choices taken away from them, sometimes by well-intentioned staff.

Every Thursday Jack went to the local day centre. In the mornings staff rushed to get Jack ready for the minibus. They passed him his coat, put on his shoes and ushered him to the door. They helped him onto the bus and waved goodbye. Staff said that, as they knew Jack so well, they no longer needed to ask what he wanted.

Any opportunity for communication is pre-empted by a worker's actions. Many such opportunities are lost because the staff feel that as they know him so well they no longer feel the need to ask. Jack may be able to use these opportunities to communicate whether he wants to go or not, for example by fetching his coat or not putting on his shoes.

The following example highlights the importance of looking at the environment in which someone lives in order to create increased opportunities for making choices.

Carlos moved to England four years ago from a Spanish speaking country. Carlos used very few words, and used both Spanish and

English words when speaking. Initially staff tried to teach Carlos only English words, which he found difficult.

Staff realised that by allowing Carlos to use both languages his ability to make choices and, therefore, his independence can be increased. For example, staff recognise that Carlos says 'si' for yes and so they also say 'si' for yes when they are talking to him. Carlos has also gained more confidence and abilities in communication by recording himself on a karaoke machine.

Evaluating outcomes

Once a decision has been made and acted on it will be necessary to review the process, and ensure that the desired outcome has been reached. One health authority involved in the research had set up a project whose aim was to support individuals whose services were no longer appropriate or meeting their assessed needs. The project was set up for financial reasons, as it was found that some people were costing the service more than had been contractually agreed. After changes had been implemented, there was no system of review to check that the changes were appropriate or what the individual wanted. As in many situations, service changes are led by the needs of the service rather than those of the individuals receiving services.

The following example describes how two people gained control over how they spend their time. Jane was in her mid-twenties and lived at home with her mother. David, Jane's friend, also lived at home with his mother. They became friends at the day centre, and enjoyed spending time together. Recognising how they communicated their likes, dislikes and preferences was fundamental to them having control over how their money is spent. The story illustrates how their choices influenced decisions about what they did during the day, how they were supported, and how these changes were funded. The outcome, that they were both now satisfied with their new service arrangement was taken as evidence that decisions made reflected their wishes.

Sometimes people are satisfied with the outcomes of decisions made by others, even if they do not control the decision-making process. However, controlling decision-making is not just about outcomes but also about how and why decisions are reached. In addition to satisfaction with outcomes, there must therefore be evidence that someone has been effectively involved in the decision-making process. Only then it is possible to demonstrate that they are in control of decisions.

Jane does not use verbal communication and she will show people what she wants in a variety of ways. Two years ago Jane started refusing to take part in activities, attendance dropped to about 25%. At the same time there was a sudden change in Jane's behaviour at home and the day centre. In one month there were 36 reported incidences of hair pulling and biting at the day centre.

Her mother did not initially realise that Jane was communicating something through her behaviour. She thought that her daughter may have been unwell, or that it was something to do with her learning difficulty. It took several months for her mother to realise that Jane's change in behaviour was a result of a number of changes to the way day services were provided. Staff at the centre said that Jane did not want to get involved in activities offered. A similar pattern had happened with David. The two mothers, who met because of their son and daughter's friendship, had been able to discuss with each other possible interpretations.

Up until this point Jane and David had followed a traditional route, from school into existing local day services. It seemed likely that they would both go on to a residential care placement. In this case, Jane and David's dislike of services offered an opportunity to change the way they received services. The social worker started to look at new creative ways to deliver the services that Jane and David wanted. Over two months, Jane, David, their mothers and staff were involved in assessing her needs, abilities and wishes.

"I feel that the balance has changed from challenging parts of a service, to that of a service challenging Jane"

Jane's mother

They also had to think about new ways of funding day activities because the day centre option was so obviously inappropriate for Jane and David's needs. An application was made to the Independent Living Fund who agreed to pay some of the care package, along with the direct payments from Social Services. The agreed amount was going to cost less than what was already being spent and it was an opportunity to develop totally individualised support for Jane and David. They used this funding for two days per week. They both continued attending the day centre for two other days, with a view to evaluating this arrangement in the future.

Jane and David's direct payments are managed on their behalf by a user-controlled trust fund. They control the decision-making over how the money is spent to meet their needs for support during the day. They choose their support workers and direct how those people work with them. Jane and David choose to spend some time together and combine part of their direct payments to enable them to do things together as friends.

Once the new arrangements were started, Jane's attendance at the day centre for the scheduled two days a week rose from 25% to 98%. Reports of physical harm dropped from 36 in one month to three in four months. This was taken as evidence that the new services offered were responding to what she wanted. This is good evidence that Jane is in control: she is directly involved in choosing her new support service and her satisfaction with the arragnements is continually monitored.

Documenting decisions

Not all documentation that is written about people will be correct or up to date. For example, one participant had records from when he moved from a long stay hospital. The records were supposed to cover the last seven years, although the entire report had been written by one member of staff a couple of weeks before the individual moved out. Given the importance that documentation can play in demonstrating how decisions have been reached it is essential that records are kept up to date and accurate.

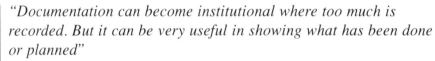

"Documentation can become institutional where too much is recorded. But it can be very useful in showing what has been done or planned"

Residential Home Manager

Risk

The approach to risk in someone's life will give an indication of whether they are being supported to make choices and be in control of their lives. Life involves risk. New challenges and experiences, and the opportunity to grow through them, involve risk. People should be enabled to take risks in their lives. The focus needs to be less on risk and more on safeguards.

Supporting people to try new things and even make mistakes should be documented too. Risk assessments can be one way of doing this. They are intended to be used to protect the health and safety of individuals who are being supported by services. Risk assessments should be seen as a way of facilitating people's involvement in different activities or situations by identifying what safeguards are needed to enable them to take part positively. Safeguards are about positive forethought, not about infringing someone's right to self-determination and autonomy.

In practice, staff in a number of research sites were more likely to use risk assessments to protect themselves and their organisations from claims of negligence. This approach is more likely to reduce people's experiences and opportunities. People are not 'allowed' to do certain activities because they are perceived as too risky or to support someone is seen as too difficult. In some cases there is no legal basis to not 'allowing' someone to take risks and services may even be acting illegally by infringing people's legal rights to choice (see chapter 4).

The existence of a risk assessment is not necessarily evidence that someone is in control. In some cases it could be evidence to the contrary. For example, staff supporting Carlos had completed a number of assessments about potential risks in and out of the home. Early risk assessments had been written by the service manager and then agreed by his uncle, as next of kin (although there was no legal basis to his uncle's position as representative - see chapter 4). The focus had been on protecting the organisation from negligence rather than allowing Carlos to do things that might be seen as risky. More recent assessments have involved Carlos himself, in addition to a number of other people including the manager, his uncle, support staff and his advocate. The emphasis is now on trying to find ways that will allow Carlos to take part in these activities, rather than preventing him from doing so.

Summary

This chapter has looked at the different ways in which someone's choices and preferences can control how decisions reached. The examples given in this section underline the significance of people having access to good support and opportunities in order to be in control of decisions.

- Record how people communicate their likes, dislikes and preferences.
- Use these choices to influence how decisions are made.
- Provide information in a variety of formats.
- Try things out.
- Challenge assumptions about how someone communicates.
- Work in a person-centred way – seeing each person as an individual.

LEGAL ISSUES 4

This chapter will outline the present legal situation concerning decision-making by and with people who have learning difficulties. Each of the three main areas of legal decision-making (welfare, finance and health) will be discussed. VIA's concerns over the effectiveness of proposed changes to the law in England and Wales, and new legislation in Scotland, will be discussed. The role of assessments used to ascertain whether someone is legally able to make a particular decision will be critically evaluated.

Some decisions have legal implications or potentially significant consequences for the individual concerned, such as medical treatment and procedures, financial decisions, entering into contracts, sexual relationships.

Mental capacity is a legal concept; it is 'all-or-nothing' in that the law assumes that someone either has the capacity to make a particular decision or they do not. This does not reflect how decisions are made by any of us in real life. People with learning difficulties can find that their ability or 'mental capacity' to make decisions about these things may be questioned, often because of generalised assumptions made about them, the way they communicate or the labels they have been given.

However, Common Law incorporates a presumption of capacity. This means that everyone, including people with learning difficulties, is presumed to be able to make decisions for themselves, until proved otherwise. For many people with learning difficulties, the opposite is often the reality: they are presumed to be incapable of making their own decisions until they pass some unspecified 'test' to prove that they can. Staff and supporters should use the presumption of capacity as their starting point, assuming that everyone has the legal capacity - and therefore legal right - to make their own choices and supporting them to do so.

Common Law also judges capacity for each particular decision at each moment in time. Many people with learning difficulties find that the labels and reputations given to them in the past influence assumptions about their abilities and capacities in the present. Staff should be wary about the reputations that precede people and use the Common Law situation to support their own efforts to enable someone to make their own choices. For example, the fact that someone has an 'appointee' to manage their Social Security benefits on their behalf does not indicate whether they are currently able to be in control of their direct payment.

VIA works from the premise that all human beings can be supported to be in control of their lives. However, if someone is found to be legally 'incapable' of making a particular decision then they may find their right to make their own decisions taken away from them. This may happen even when someone is actually legally capable of making his or her own decisions because of widespread assumptions and misunderstanding about the law on decision-making. Other people may be given substitute decision-making powers. Change to the law in Scotland, and proposed change in England and Wales, suggests that substitute decisions should be made with regard to 'best interests principles'. However, there is virtually no monitoring of, or challenge to, substitute decision-making and very little protection of the individual's interests. This is discussed in more detail below.

Decisions that have legal implications are guided by case law, which defines when someone is legally capable or incapable of making a particular decision (a summary of key legal cases is given in appendix C). The absence of legislation and little guidance around decision-making has created a situation where many people with learning difficulties are being denied their right to make decisions they could legally make for themselves (Bewley, 1998).

There can be a tendency to call in for professional help in the form of a community learning disability team, psychologist or GP when faced with controversial or difficult dilemmas. Some staff involved in the research stated that they would sometimes call in such professionals without really knowing what they wanted. A psychologist involved in the research said that referrals were difficult when it was not clear why they were being asked to be involved. This response may well result in people being labeled as 'mentally incapable' of making a particular decision, this label then being applied to all decision-making situations.

This research found that current practice tended to be 'when it's a controversial issue, call in the medical people'. This response does not reflect the principle that people should "be enabled and encouraged to take for themselves those decisions which they are able to take" (Law Commission Report 231, *Mental Incapacity,* 1995). In the vast majority of situations it would be more appropriate to involve professionals to aid with *supporting* someone make a decision, rather than questioning whether someone is legally able to do so.

Welfare, financial and health decisions

As discussed in chapter 2, legal decision-making can be divided into three main categories. The following sections will outline the main differences and the legal implications.

Welfare decisions

No one is legally entitled to make welfare decisions on behalf of another adult, except where permission is given by the individual or, if the person is deemed to lack legal capacity, someone has been given authority to do so. This authority is not covered by a particular title but by a 'general authority to act' in the person's best interests. Many decisions, however, are made on a daily basis by parents, carers and support staff on behalf of people with learning difficulties. In practice, many decisions made for someone will be illegal as this 'general authority' becomes so wide that it infringes on decisions individuals could make for themselves, with or without support (Bewley, 1998).

The law is different in Scotland, where a guardian may be appointed to make what are seen as decisions affecting the person's welfare, such as where they live.

The proposed legislation for England and Wales (*Making Decisions*, see below) suggests the introduction of a 'manager' role, someone appointed by the Court of Protection who will have the power to make a wide range of decisions on behalf of a 'mentally incapable' adult, including welfare decisions.

Financial decisions

People can lose control over many decisions in their lives because other people control their money. For example, an appointee may collect Social Security benefits on behalf of another person, a trust fund may manage their finances or a receiver their assets through the Court of Protection. VIA has come across many examples of how these appointments fail to take into account the wishes of the individuals concerned. (For a detailed analysis of the specific problems associated with finances see Bewley, 1997). The case study of Jane and David in chapter 3 illustrates how people with high support needs can be in control of how money is spent even when they are not able to manage money by themselves.

Health decisions

Health professionals must seek consent from patients for all medical procedures, such as examination, diagnostic tests, and interventions aimed at alleviating or preventing the deterioration of a medical condition. At present if someone is unable to consent to medical procedures the decision can be made by medical professionals under the 'common law doctrine of necessity' (Keywood, Fovargue and Flynn, 1999). However, in practice health professionals make assessments on an instinctive or intuitive basis (Law Commission, 1991). Health professionals often adopt an 'eyeball' method of determining an individual's capacity (Morris et al, 1993).

Demonstrating that someone is in control of health decisions will involve the same process as for other decisions. Doctors who make assessments of someone's capacity to make a particular decision should be able to justify their findings. The UK needs effective systems to enable individuals or their supporters to challenge these assessments.

The legal test of capacity

One main legal test of mental capacity is the Common Law test of capacity, which considers whether at the time the decision is made the person can:

    a) understand and retain the information relevant to the decision in question;

    b) believe that information; and

    c) weigh that information in the balance to arrive at a choice.

These factors were initially defined from a case involving a man with a mental illness who refused medical treatment (*Re C. Adult: Refusal of Treatment*), and have been refined by later cases. How much information someone needs to 'weigh in the balance' depends on the severity of the outcome of the decision being made. The threshold is sufficiently low to enable people to make decisions, although it is still not clear how much information one has to understand and retain, or for how long.

The example below concerns a research participant called Ian and his involvement in medical research trails. Ian would have to understand in broad terms information about the procedure, possible risks and benefits to taking part. In legal terms, the amount of information that he would have to understand would be to a lesser degree than if he was to take part in non-therapeutic research. For non-therapeutic research he would need to understand these consequences in greater detail, because the intervention would not be directly benefiting him.

Ian had decided that he would like to take part in medical trials that were testing drugs for muscle spasticity. He had been on two trials, the first of which was partly successful, and the second had showed no improvement. He decided that he did not want to take part a third time.

As Ian has learning difficulties and does not use verbal communication his legal capacity may have been questioned. However, by providing information in a way that was understandable to Ian and exploring the possible risk, he decided to go ahead with the trials. In supporting Ian with making this possibly contentious issue staff bore in mind the following factors:

- *No one is legally entitled to make this decision on his behalf*
- *Ian must be assumed by law to have the capacity to make this decision*
- *Information is provided in ways that are meaningful to Ian*
- *Information has been given to Ian in a variety of ways*
- *Ian has been willing to take calculated risks in the past*
- *Information was provided by people that Ian trusted and knew well*
- *The views of others were taken into account about Ian's wishes and feelings*
- *This process took a number of months and there has been a consensus on how Ian communicates his preferences*

Some people are wrongly assumed to lack the capacity to make certain decisions because they have learning difficulties. The following example illustrates how someone might lose their right to make a decision if efforts were made to support them.

Joshua had expressed interest in receiving direct payments so that he could choose who supports him and when they work. Initially, he was refused direct payments as his social worker did not believe he had the capacity to consent.

This is contrary to the principle of assuming someone has legal capacity until proved otherwise. The decision about capacity was not based on any formal assessment, nor had any attempts been made to provide accessible information to Joshua. After meetings with a local advocacy group Joshua found out more information about direct payments and what it would involve. Social Services have now agreed to give him direct payments.

Assessments of 'mental capacity'

People lose their right to autonomy if deemed legally incapable, so questioning why and how assessments are carried out is crucial. Assessments of 'mental capacity' can only legally be carried out by the medical profession and refer to someone's ability to make a particular decision at a particular time. 'Mental capacity' is a purely legal concept and ultimately only Courts have the right to make a conclusive decision about someone's capacity. In practice, assessments are carried out without going to Court, although whoever is making a judgement about someone's capacity must be able to justify their decision if challenged.

Despite the importance that assessments have in determining someone's right to make a decision there is little guidance to carrying out assessments. A functional approach should be used when determining whether someone lacks capacity, which looks at whether someone is able to make a particular decision at a particular time. However, the assessment process can be flawed because assessments are often made during one short visit (Law Society and BMA, 1997), they do not involve people who know the individual well, such as parents, carers, staff and advocates, and may not provide information in an accessible way. One psychologist in this research noted that assessments have even been carried out from the individual's records alone. In addition, decisions are not always of a medical nature, therefore it is not appropriate, for example, that a GP should assess someone's ability to manage their financial affairs.

The following advice comes from Assessment of 'mental capacity' by the Law Society and British Medical Association (1995). It highlights the importance of questioning and challenging assumptions that are made about someone's capacity to make a decision.

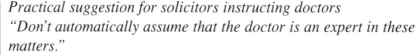

Practical suggestion for solicitors instructing doctors
"Don't automatically assume that the doctor is an expert in these matters."
Practical suggestion for doctors receiving instructions from solicitors
"Don't automatically assume that the solicitor is an expert in these matters or that he or she has told you everything you need to know."

Ways to effectively increase the control held by the individual during assessments:
- Include people who are closest to the individual, who are familiar with how someone communicates.
- Look for ways someone can be enabled to make decisions.

- Involve an independent advocate.
- Allow enough time in appropriate locations.
- Include all relevant information in a way that is accessible to the individual.
- Information from ongoing supported decisions may be useful.
- Everyone should know who is involved and what their roles are.

Appeals and complaints

It can be difficult for people with high support needs and their supporters to challenge a judgement of incapacity. Supporters often feel intimidated by the view of a doctor or psychologist and unsure how they can challenge assessments. In addition, someone with high support needs may well have difficulty accessing a complaints system or the legal system. Having been assessed as 'mentally incapable' of making decisions, they may also find they are judged as incapable of instructing a solicitor. In legal circumstances solicitors can be given instructions by another person, such as a receiver, litigation friend (formerly called 'next friend') or a guardian ad litem.

In Scotland, any appeal against a decision of incapacity would be made to the sheriff, unless the sheriff had made the decision. In that case, appeal should be made to the sheriff principal and then, with permission from the sheriff principal, to the Court of Session.

'Best interests' decision-making

Any decision made by someone who has been given the authority to do so, must be made in the individual's 'best interests'. For decisions with serious consequences the Courts will decide what is in the person's best interests. Following on from the Law Commissions proposals and consultation, the Government recommends that the following principles should be used when assessing someone's best interests (from *Making Decisions*, 1999):

a) the ascertainable past and present wishes and feelings of the person concerned and the factors the person would consider if able to do so;

b) the need to permit and encourage the person to participate or improve his or her ability to participate as fully as possible in anything done for and any decision affecting him or her;

c) the views of other people whom it is appropriate and practical to consult about the person's wishes and feelings and what would be in his or her best interests;

d) whether the purpose for which any action or decision is required can be as effectively achieved in a manner less restrictive of the person's freedom of action;

e) whether there is reasonable expectation of the person recovering capacity to make the decision in the reasonably foreseeable future;

f) the need to be satisfied that the wishes of the person were not the result of undue influence.

Using the best interests principles

The wishes and preferences of an individual should influence all decisions that are made with and for them. People with high support needs may well need substantial help in translating expressions of preference into decisions and then putting those decisions into practice. There may be occasions - for example, managing certain financial situations or instructing a solicitor - when someone has to act in a legal context on behalf of the individual. As mentioned above, these decisions can only be made by someone appointed to do so or with the permission of the individual.

There is often little critical discussion about what may be considered someone's 'best interests'. Frequently, only the views of other people seem to play a part in decisions that are supposedly made in someone's best interests. This is highlighted by a number of recent cases (such as *F v West Berkshire Health Authority or Re MB medical treatment*) where only the opinion of other people is taken into consideration. If people have been deemed unable to make a decision it does not mean that they do not have any views on the matter. Solicitors and barristers should ask more frequently whether the person has been given support to make these decisions before they reach Court (by which time it may be too late) and for evidence of their preferences and wishes and how these have been used to direct decision-making.

Law reform in England and Wales

The Law Commission in England and Wales spent five years looking at the law in the area of decision-making on behalf of people who lack 'mental capacity'. From four consultation papers the Law Commission presented its recommendations for legal reform to the Government (Law Commission Report 231, *Mental Incapacity*, 1995). In 1997 the Government published a Green Paper called *Who Decides? Making Decisions on Behalf of Mentally Incapacitated Adults* (Lord Chancellor's Department, 1997).

Who Decides? was a consultation document allowing people to respond to the proposals. The Lord Chancellor's Department received over 4000 responses from organisations and individuals. The range of these responses highlights the controversial nature and different opinions on the subject.

In October 1999, the Government published a Position Paper (the document that appears before a White Paper or Bill) called *Making Decisions*, the Government's proposals for making decisions on behalf of mentally incapacitated adults (Lord Chancellor's Department, 1999). Since this time no further developments have been made. The Lord Chancellor has stated that a Bill will be presented 'when Parliamentary time can found'.

Many people involved in the research were unaware of the legal situation around decision-making or the proposed changes. Staff highlighted the need for information about rights and legislation. Some residential homes maintain a library of resources, while others provide little information. One organisation has an internal newsletter from the Head Office that keeps people updated on policy and practice developments. But most staff were given no information about people's legal rights to make decisions.

People covered by the legislation

Making Decisions (1999) proposes a new statutory definition of incapacity, which states that a person will be judged as 'mentally incapable' of making a decision for him/herself if, at the time the decision needs to be taken, they are unable to do so due to mental disability or inability to communicate the decision. Mental disability is defined as 'any disability or disorder of the mind or brain, whether permanent or temporary, which results in an impairment or disturbance of functioning'. Mental disability could result in someone being unable to understand or retain relevant information or use it to make a decision.

This definition does not necessarily promote better assessments of 'mental capacity' or better practice in enabling every individual to participate in decision-making. There will need to be effective guidance for those conducting assessments about how they should interpret what 'relevant information' is required or what lengths they should go to so that what someone is communicating is understood. The difficulty with such definitions is that they are meant to cover a wide range of people, including those who are unconscious and therefore unable to consent to life-saving treatment and those who lose decision-making abilities in later life. This proposed legal definition of 'mental capacity' has not been designed to properly address the life experience of people with learning difficulties who have high support needs, their ability to communicate through words, sounds and behaviour, and the skills of those supporting them.

How far the proposals for legal change in England and Wales will go to protect people's rights to make their own decisions has yet to be seen. There needs to be a stronger emphasis on 'all practicable steps being taken to enable a person to communicate their decisions' (Making Decisions, 1999). The practice guidance will need to consider what are 'all practicable steps'? What resources are available to do this? Who will make sure that people are supported to make decisions? How can people complain if they think 'all practicable steps' have not been taken?

Similarly, VIA is concerned about the extension of the Court of Protection's role and the extension of the 'manager' role (Bewley, 1998). These proposals would give people who now act as receivers vastly extended rights to make decisions over health and social welfare matters, without rigourous proposals for monitoring and challenging those in this 'manager' role. The 'best interests' proposals in *Making Decisions* suggest a process of decision-making in keeping with the good practice guidelines in this report but these are not backed up by an effective monitoring or complaints system. It is therefore unclear whether the proposed legal changes will have a positive effect on enabling people with learning difficulties who have high support needs to be more in control of the decisions affecting their lives.

New legislation in Scotland

New legislation around decision-making on behalf of adults who lack capacity has been introduced in Scotland: the *Adults with Incapacity (Scotland) Act 2000*. The law in this area has historically differed from the rest of the UK, and what follows is a brief description of the previous and new legal situations.

In the past, people who lived in long-stay hospitals in Scotland were legally defined as 'incapax' and were deemed not to have the capacity to make decisions. This outrageous and de-humanising label was applied across the board to long-stay hospital residents with learning difficulties. It meant that these people were legally assumed totally to lack capacity to make decisions and their rights to do so were thus taken away from them. This label was never applied to people living in the community, although it continues to be used illegally to prevent people living in community settings from making decisions. For example, the fact that someone used to live in long-stay hospital and was therefore labeled 'incapax' has been wrongly used to justify preventing them from entering tenancy contracts.

Scotland has a system of substitute decision-making about finances that allows for the appointment of a 'curator bonis', a person who is allowed to manage someone's finances on their behalf. The curator bonis is often a solicitor or accountant and has a duty to take account of the person's wishes and act in his or her best interests. However, the experience of people involved in the research in Scotland suggests that financial decisions were made with little or no consultation either with the individual (called a 'ward') or their supporters (Bewley, 1997).

This situation will not be remedied when the new Adults with Incapacity Act's intervention and guardianship orders are implemented in 2002. A curator bonis will then be regarded as a financial guardian but will continue to have absolute power over financial decisions. Their duties will be subject to supervision by the public guardian rather than the accountant of the Sheriff's Court. New guardianship appointments made after April 2002 will, however, be given specific short-term powers, for example to sell a house.

Anyone can apply to be a guardian and the Court must decide if they are suitable. If no one is available then the Court can act on an individual's behalf. Guardianship appointments can be revoked in a number of circumstances. Challenges can be made by the individual or anyone with an interest, so can include independent advocates, family, and friends.

Definitions of mental capacity in Scotland

An incapable adult, according to the *Adults with Incapacity (Scotland) Act 2000*, is defined as someone who is 16 years or over and, by reason of mental disorder or physical disability, is incapable of the following:

    a) acting; or

    b) making decisions; or

c) communicating decisions; or

d) understanding decisions; or

e) retaining the memory of decisions.

This definition is wide-ranging and vague, a recipe for an even more restrictive assessment of 'mental capacity'. The definition puts the burden on the individual to act, communicate, understand and otherwise 'prove' their capacity to make decisions, rather than emphasising the roles of the supporter and assessor in enabling people to make decisions for themselves. Left to the interpretation of medical and legal systems which may understand little about current good practice in enabling people to be in control of their own lives, this definition may well limit the opportunities and legal rights of those who find themselves defined by it.

Implementation of the Adults with Incapacity (Scotland) Act 2000

April 2001

- The Office of the Public Guardian will be set up.
- Provisions for continuing and welfare attorneys will begin.
- Provisions for the access to funds scheme will begin.

Summer 2001

- Medical treatment and research will start to be covered by the Act.

September 2001

- Provisions for the management of residents' finances will begin.

April 2002

- Intervention and Guardianship orders will begin.

Summary

This chapter highlighted the proposed legislation in England and Wales and new legislation in Scotland, concerning decision-making. VIA's concerns were expressed over how far the legislation will go to protect the rights of everyone to make their own decisions.

- Everyone must be assumed to have the capacity to make a particular decision unless proved otherwise.
- People must be enabled to make their own decisions by having the opportunities and support to make choices.
- People only need to have a broad understanding of the proposed decision and understand possible consequences to reach a decision. People with learning difficulties should not be expected to make decisions better than anyone else.
- Someone must not be assumed to lack the legal capacity on the basis of the decision itself. People have a legal right to make what others may see as 'foolish' decisions.
- "All practicable steps must be taken to enable a person without capacity to communicate their decisions" (Making Decisions 1999)

CONCLUSIONS 5

The ideas presented in this report are deceptively simple. Good communication, effective working relationships, supporting people to participate, giving people choice: there is surely no debate in contemporary service provision about whether these factors are essential to good decision-making. Yet VIA's research over the last decade has persistently shown that people with learning difficulties do not have the range of ordinary life choices that other people take for granted. Many people have only minimal and superficial control over their own lives. This is not due to the fact that people have learning difficulties or high support needs. It is something to do with the structure of services and the ways in which we support people that restricts their legal and moral rights to self-determination.

VIA's research into decision-making began with the belief that everyone can communicate their likes, dislikes and preferences in some way, and that everyone can be supported to be in control of their own lives. These principles raise the questions 'how can we support someone to be in control of their lives?' and, for people with learning difficulties who have high support needs, 'how do we know if self-determination has been achieved?'. What would the evidence look like?

Some people might find VIA's original premise problematic. What about people with complex and challenging support needs, people who do not use speech who have very limited capacity to understand the issues involved in decision-making? What about people who are judged as 'mentally incapable' of making their own decisions and who therefore may not have the legal right to self-determination in some legal situations?

Chapters 2 and 3 addressed the first of these problematic questions. By emphasising effective communication and systematic teamwork, and by giving people more choice and more control, this project has shown how people can be at the very heart of all decision-making.

The legal situation was described and analysed in chapter 4. Current Common Law in England and Wales lacks rigour in its processes of assessment of capacity and substitute decision-making. Indeed, the current legal approach to 'mental capacity' and its interpretation within service provision usually takes away opportunity for choice, control and self-determination from people with learning difficulties, especially those with high support needs. Existing systems of substitute decision-making have not, on the whole, enabled people with learning difficulties to take control of the decision-making processes around their lives; in fact they have often done the opposite.

New legislation in Scotland and new proposals in England and Wales assume that substitute decision-makers need no effective training, guidance, monitoring or challenge. Legal developments are naïve in this sense and, despite including positive elements such as guidance on 'best interests' decision-making, there is no promise that they will greatly shift the balance of power between people with learning difficulties and those who support them or make decisions with and for them.

What about the second of these 'problematic' questions: how do we know if self-determination has been achieved? What would evidence of control look like? VIA has resisted the temptation to write a checklist for such evidence. A key lesson from the project is that decision-making with someone who has high support needs is an on-going process that requires good partnerships, relationships and communication to succeed. It is not appropriate to dictate what these partnerships, relationships and forms of communication should look like for each individual. It is all too easy for a checklist to become a straightjacket.

However, this research has found that there are factors which, if present, strongly indicate that someone is being supported to achieve self-determination and to be in control of their life. If factors from the following list are present and if they are shown to be integral parts of everyday life, then there is evidence that an individual is controlling or determining decisions, even if they require substantial support to make choices and implement them.

Factors that provide evidence of an individual controlling their own life

- Individual themselves are involved in choice and decision-making at all times, in ways that proactively enhance their participation.
- Imaginative, effective ways of communicating with people are used as a matter of course.
- A range of people are involved in, and may even share a responsibility for, decision-making.
- There is clear evidence of collaborative teamwork from staff and other supporters, including collective responsibility for recording evidence.
- Decision-making systems may be formalised into circles of support or user-controlled trust funds.
- Proactive efforts are made to maximise the range of options available to people and to enable them to actively live in, and belong to, ordinary communities.
- Participation is enhanced by using simple, appropriate language, accessible information and by creating suitable decision-making environments.
- Control is viewed as a process that involves everyone, not a 'test' that the individual has to pass.
- This process is clearly recorded in detail, using imaginative methods where possible (e.g. photographs, pictures, multi-media etc.) and shared by those involved in helping the person make choices.

- Decisions, their outcomes and the individual's satisfaction with them are reviewed regularly.
- There is an easy-to-use system by which others can question the decision-making process and its outcomes. A formal complaints system should also be in place.
- People's legal right to make their own choices and take control of their lives is respected and promoted.
- Everyone works from the presumption that the person can legally consent to, and control, decisions.
- Everyone takes active steps to enhance the person's capacity to formally and legally make their own decisions.
- Formal assessments of capacity are used rarely and with great caution. They are not used simply to 'pass-the-buck' when there are contentious or difficult choices.

Those wanting to promote choice and control for people with learning difficulties, and those wanting to check whether someone is in control, should look for evidence of the above factors.

People need choice and control. Recognising a person's preferences is the first step, and acknowledging them as indicative of choice is the second, but outcomes are important too. Where is someone living? How is their life? Are they happy? Is there a clear and direct link between their views, preferences and choices and the life they are living? Is the decision-making process explicit, recorded and justifiable? If not, then it appears that someone else is in control of that individual's life.

'Who's in control?' is a question that is fundamentally about power: the balance of power between those who need support to live their lives and those who provide, fund and organise that support. A simple focus on choice is not enough: the answer to 'who's in control?' will often turn out to be 'someone else'. We need a new definition of self-determination that does not restrict the opportunities for choice and control to those who can pass intellectual tests of 'mental capacity'; a new definition that states every human being's right to self-determination and the support they need to achieve this. If we operated our legal system and service structures from this perspective, we might reach a different answer to the question 'who's in control?'.

6 APPENDICES

Appendix A

Methodology

This research project took place between August 1999 and January 2001. Fifteen participants from England and Scotland took part in the research over an eight-month period. Participants were from one of four research sites selected according to geographical location i.e. rural and urban areas, and specifically Scotland because of the difference in legislation. Nine homes were selected (some of the participants lived together) to reflect different support arrangements, i.e. residential care, independent living, and living at home with parents. Each participant and their supporters were visited on a number of occasions over a two-month period. Participants were visited again towards the end of the project.

Consent was sought from all the participants throughout the project. Initial visits were made prior to taking part in the research in order to explain what the project was about and what taking part involved.

Area 1:

Small independent support agency in Scotland

Three participants lived in houses managed by a housing association in Scotland. They were being supported by a small independent support agency. Two of the participants, Ian and Nina, lived together with three other people. Ian had been involved in a number of decisions concerning living independently and taking part in medical research trails. Practical and emotional support had been given to Nina while she was in a long-term relationship. One participant, Paul, was supported to live independently and faced many new decisions about his future.

Area 2:

Independent residential care home provision in Southern England

Four participants lived in two residential homes owned and managed by an independent support agency in the South of England. Two participants, Ralph and Beverley, lived in the same house together with three other people. Ralph was involved in a number of decisions about what he did during the day. Beverley and Ralph both communicated non-verbally, in ways that required careful interpretation.

Two other participants, Alex (not referred to by name in the report) and Jack lived in the same house with four other people. Jack was trying out new activities during the day, as he did not appear to enjoy going to the day centre.

Area 3:
Independent living and support in an English rural county

Two participants, David and Jane, lived with their families and directly controlled their day opportunities using direct payments (via a user-controlled trust fund), Independent Living Fund (ILF) and Social Security benefits. Both of their mothers and members of the Social Services Department were interviewed in order to establish the ways in which the two participants were in control of how the money is spent.

Also from this area were two people, Daniel and Joshua, who received support from independent advocates. These two participants, their advocates and others took part in a small group discussion to look at the role advocacy can play in making decisions. Daniel had current concerns relating to his support worker. Joshua was interested in receiving direct payments. Members of the Social Service Department were also interviewed to see how advocacy affected their practice.

Area 4:
Person-centred planning in an English NHS Trust

Four participants received home support from a large health authority. The authority had carried out Essential Lifestyle Planning (a person-centred planning tool) to find out what the people who used their services wanted. Staff and managers were beginning to implement some of these plans according to the wishes of the individuals. Two participants, Michelle and Lucy, had lived together in a converted bungalow for about eight years. Both women had ELP's that had enabled staff to build up a better picture of how Michelle and Lucy communicated their likes and dislikes.

Two additional participants, Martin and Carlos, lived with others in neighbouring residential homes. Martin was faced with the prospect of being moved, complicated by differences of opinion about where he wanted to live. Carlos moved to England about four years ago from a Spanish speaking country.

Appendix B

Protecting people's rights

Human Rights Act 1998

The Human Rights Act 1998 (HRA) came into force on October 2nd 2000. It is an important piece of UK legislation because it represents the first time that basic human rights are listed in primary legislation in the UK. Prior to the HRA people had to take cases to the European Court of Human Rights in Strasbourg, after first failing to find a remedy in domestic courts. This process was often long, expensive and difficult. Very few cases involving people with learning difficulties reached the European Court of Human Rights. The HRA now means that legal challenges based on human rights principles can be made in all domestic courts across the UK.

Some possible areas in which the HRA may be directly relevant will be in challenging assessments of capacity, voluntary detention, use of medication, issues around abuse and use of resources. Most cases that go to Court can be considered in light of the Human Rights legislation. The HRA only covers public authorities, for example, the Courts, local authorities, social and health services and the police. However, as the Courts are also covered by the Act they have a duty to ensure that their own procedures do not infringe people's rights in relation to private matters.

The HRA has many implications about decision-making by people with learning difficulties. The Articles that may have the biggest impact for people with learning difficulties are listed below with some examples of areas in which they could be used.

Article 3 - prohibition on inhuman and degrading treatment
- Abuse or degrading treatment in residential homes, day centres, and hospitals.
- Compulsory medical treatment.
- Standards of community care.

Article 5 - right to liberty, lawful detention and review of detention
- Use of 'time out' to deal with 'challenging behaviour'.
- Being informally detained in hospital without consent.
- Being detained without review of purpose of detention.

Article 6 (1) - the right to a fair trial
- Lack of support or special measures within the Court system.
- Tribunal decisions, for example about social security.

Article 8 - the protection of private life
- Removal of children from the family home by local authorities.
- Decisions about someone's legal capacity to make decisions.
- Provision of facilities to give disabled people access to places where they can develop relationships.

Article 10 – freedom of expression
- whether a decision allows for someone to express their views and to

receive information about the decision.

- complaints procedures for people who use services.
- perhaps strengthen people's right to receive information in an accessible form.

Article 12 - the right to marry

- Sterilisation of women with learning difficulties.
- Denial of fertility treatment on the grounds of disability.

Article 14 - the right not to be discriminated against

- Assumptions made about people's right to make decisions.
- Different treatment of parents with learning difficulties.
- Unequal protection against assault.
- Implied right to access services, e.g. leisure services.

Complaints procedures

People with learning difficulties should have access to an accessible complaints procedure, so they can appeal against decisions made by service organisations. A number of organisations involved in this research made complaints procedures available in a variety of formats, such as on tape, and in easy words and pictures. Organisations also need to be aware of how people are communicating that something is wrong or that they wish to challenge decisions that are taken. People should be to be able to access the complaints procedure even when they are unable to verbally express this wish. In this respect, an independent advocate can be very important when investigating claims.

Access to records

Records play a key part in decision-making. It is therefore vital that people have access to their records to ensure they are accurate and up to date. People now have a legal access to any information that is kept on computer or paper under the Data Protection Act 1998. This Act replaces much of what was formerly covered in the Access to Personal Files Act 1987 and Access to Health Records Act 1990. People can ask for their own files or others can ask for the records with the consent of the individual concerned. Some parts of records may not be seen, such as where third parties are mentioned. If access is denied the organisation holding the record must say on what grounds they have been refused. Challenges should be made firstly to the organisation that is holding the records to reconsider its decision. If this is unsuccessful then cases can be taken to the Parliamentary Ombudsman or Scottish Parliamentary Ombudsman.

Disability Discrimination Act 1995

People can have their choices restricted by discrimination within services. The Disability Discrimination Act 1995 (DDA) aims to protect the rights of disabled people and covers anyone involved in providing any kinds of goods, facilities or services to the public (unless exempted), those selling, renting or managing land or property, and those involved in the area of employment (unless exempted).

Discrimination can occur where:

- a disabled person is treated less favourably than someone else;
- the treatment is for a reason relating to the person's disability and this treatment can't be justified;
- there is a failure to make a reasonable adjustment for a disabled person and that failure cannot be justified.

More information can be found from the DDA Helpline (see 'contacts' section).

Appendix C
Relevant case law

A person's legal capacity to make a particular decision can ultimately only be decided by the Courts. In practice, judgements of someone's capacity will be made on a daily basis without going to Court but professionals must be able to justify their assessments of capacity is challenged. Cases that do get to Court usually concern decisions that have serious consequences, such as medical interventions. The following examples outline some of the key cases that have defined and interpreted the law around 'mental capacity' and decision-making.

Male sterilisation case – Re A

A mother of a 28 year old man with Down's syndrome was concerned that as her health declined she would be unable to supervise A, and he might make a woman pregnant. The mother wanted her son to be sterilised in his 'best interests'. The Official Solicitor opposed this declaration. The declaration was refused on the grounds that although A was sexually aware, the benefits of a vasectomy were unclear, the chances of A having a sexual relationship was low and the effect upon A of any possible pregnancy was minimal.

Re A (Male Sterilisation) Re (2000) 1 FLR 549, CA

Bournewood case

The Bournewood 'case' concerned a middle-aged man with learning difficulties in England who became distressed whilst attending a day centre. Following a series of decisions made by day centre staff, a doctor and a social worker he was removed to the 'learning disability' hospital where he used to live. He was admitted as an *informal* patient under the Mental Health Act 1983 because he was deemed mentally incapable of either consenting or refusing the proposed treatment. Due to the assumption of incapacity he was not afforded the right to a second opinion, appeal or review given to people who are detained *formally* under the Mental Health Act.

The man's carers objected to his admission and the man himself displayed clear evidence of his continued distress at his detention. However, the consultant psychiatrist refused to release him and so his carers challenged this decision as being manifestly not 'in his best interests'. The case proceeded to the House of Lords, where the Law Lords ruled in favour of the hospital but, in their judgement, criticised the actions of the hospital and the current law about decision-making for people deemed to lack capacity to consent. The case has since been taken to the European Court of Human Rights (House of Lords, 1997-1998).

Dispute over access – Re D-R

In this case the courts had to consider whether access by a family member to a person with a learning difficulty was in the person's 'best interests'.

Re D - R (Contact: mentally incapacitatedadult) [1999] 2 FCR 49, CA

Mental patient and sterilisation – Re F

This case was the first to be considered after the power of 'guardians' (under the Mental Health Act 1959) to consent to medical treatment on behalf of someone with learning difficulties or mental health problems were abolished (after the introduction of the Mental Health Act 1983). While this case concerned sterilisation, the ruling of the House of Lords applies to consent to any kind of physical contact.

F v West Berkshire Health Authority (1990) 2 AC 1,
sub nom F (sterilisation: mental patient) Re (1989) 2 FLR 376, HL

Adult patient and medical treatment – Re SL

This case is important because it attempts to clarify how the 'best interests' guidelines should be applied. It clarifies the position of the Courts to make a final determination of someone's best interests, rather than health professionals or parents who may have different ideas about someone's best interests. Problems had arisen in cases after Re F because some judges were allowing professionals to determine what was in the 'best interests' of someone with a learning difficulty. Courts were unprepared to intervene, and so in effect decisions were not always being made in someone's best interests.

Re SL (adult patient: medical treatment) (2000) 1 FCR 361

Declaration against parents – Re V

A child with cerebral palsy was prevented from developing because of his mother's 'over-protective attitude towards him'. The local authority applied for a care order that was granted. V wanted a declaration against his parents stating that when he legally became an adult, he was entitled to decide for himself 'where he lived and with whom he associated'.

Re V (Declaration against parents) Re (1995) 2 FLR 1003

Key

CA – Court of Appeal
FD – Family Division
FCR – Family Court Report
FLR – Family Law Reporter
FLR – House of Lords

Appendix D

Contacts

Acting Up for information on Multimedia Profiling
Telephone 020 7275 9173

Advocacy 2000 (Scotland) for further information about advocacy
contact them at 134 Ferry Road, Edinburgh EH6 4PQ
Telephone 0131 554 7878

CHANGE (London) an organisation of people with learning difficulties and
sensory impairment
Telephone 020 7490 2668

CHANGE North a branch of Change based in Leeds
Telephone 0113 243 0202

Circles Network an organisation that promotes, supports and coordinates
circles of support around the country
Telephone 0117 9393 917 (Bristol) or visit www.circlesnetwork.org.uk

Citizen Advocacy Information & Training
162 Lee Valley Technopark, Ashley Road, London N17 9LN
Telephone 020 8880 4545 or visit www.leevalley.co.uk/cait

Department of Health
Richmond House, 79 Whitehall, London SW1A 2NS
Telephone 020 7210 4850

Disability Discrimination Act Helpline
DDA Help, Freepost MIDO2164, Stratford upon Avon, CV37 9BR
Telephone 0345 622 633 or visit www.disability.gov.uk

Disability Rights Commission (DRC)
Telephone 0845 7622 633

Foundation for People with Learning Disabilities
Telephone 020 7535 7400

Joseph Rowntree Foundation
Telephone 01904 629 241 or visit www.jrf.org.uk

Justice for information about the Human Rights Act 1998
Telephone 020 7329 5100 or visit www.justice.org.uk

Law Society
Telephone 020 7242 1222

Legal Services Agency (Scotland)
Telephone 0141 353 3354 or 0131 228 9993

Lord Chancellor's Department
Selbourne House, 54 - 60 Victoria Street, London SW1E 6QW

National Centre for Independent Living
250 Kennington Lane, London SE11 5RD
Telephone 0207 587 1663

Norah Fry Research Centre
3 Priory Road, Bristol BS8 1TX
Telephone 0117 923 8137

Pavilion Publishing
Telephone 01273 623222

People First (London) an organisation of people who have learning difficulties
3rd Floor, 299 Kentish Town Road, London NW5 2TJ
Telephone 020 7485 6660

People First (Scotland)
34b Haddington Place, Edinburgh EH7 4AG
Telephone 0131 478 7707

Public Law Project aims to improve access to the law
Telephone 020 7467 9800

RNIB
Telephone 020 7388 1266 or visit www.rnib.org.uk

Royal College of Psychiatrists produce series called Books Beyond Words
Telephone 020 7235 2351 or visit www.rcpsych.ac.uk

Scottish Executive
St Andrews House, Regent Road, Edinburgh EH1 3DG

Values Into Action
Telephone 020 7729 5436 or visit www.viauk.org
In Scotland telephone 0141 420 3655

Appendix E

Glossary

Advocacy

Independent advocacy has a number of roles in supporting people in the decision-making process. Independent advocates have no vested interests in the service or legal systems and solely represent the individual, not relatives, friends or professionals, thus avoiding conflicts of interest.

Best Interests

The Law Commission for England and Wales recommended a new general requirement to act in the 'best interests' of the person.

Choice

The option of saying 'yes' or 'no' to something, or selecting between a number of options.

Consent

The legal agreement to a choice or action made by an individual. In a legal context, the individual must be 'mentally capable' of giving consent before it is valid.

Control

Having autonomy and power over your own life and what happens to you, regardless of how much support you need to put your choices into action. Having self-determination.

Decision

The final result of a process of choosing, guiding the action that follows. The word 'decision' is also used in legal contexts.

Decision-making

The process of making choices which lead to decisions and action.

Direct Payments

Direct payments are payments made by a local authority to an individual for them to purchase the support they need, instead of the local authority providing that support.

Good Practice

Good practice means going beyond what is required by legislation. Some principles of good practice will be considered legally in judicial review and by ombudsmen when investigating maladministration. Others are described in government policy and practice guidance.

Green Paper

A Green Paper is the summary of proposals by the Government about new or amended laws. The Green Paper concerned with making decisions is called 'Who Decides? Making decisions on behalf of mentally incapacitated adults' (1997).

High support needs

The phrase used to indicate when someone needs significant support to live their daily lives.

Incapacity

Legally defined as "unable by reason of mental disability to make a decision on the matter in question; or unable to communicate a decision on that matter because he or she is unconscious or for any other reason" (Making Decisions, 1999).

Independent

Being independent means being in control of your life, whatever support you need. This contrasts with a medical definition which focuses on physical impairments and implies that independence means doing everything for yourself.

Informed choice

The option of indicating 'yes' or 'no' to something, or selecting between a number of options, when you have considered how the choices will affect you.

Judicial review

Courts supervise decisions and actions of public bodies, such as local authorities, by judicial review. Courts will consider challenges about decisions made by public bodies on the grounds of unreasonableness, unfairness and illegality.

Making Decisions

The name of the position paper produced by the Lord Chancellor's Department as a result of the consultation document, 'Who Decides? Making decisions on behalf of mentally incapacitated adults' (1997).

Mental disability

Is defined by the Law Commission (1995) as "any disability or disorder of the mind or brain, whether permanent or temporary, which results in an impairment or disturbance of mental functioning".

Policy guidance

Sets out what local authorities must do when implementing new legislation.

Practice guidance

Provides more detail about how a local authority can go about implementing different parts of new legislation.

Preference

An individual's choices and wishes, often expressed through their behaviour. Preferences are the core building blocks of a proactive decision-making process that demonstrates that an individual is determining their own life.

Service

Health, housing or social care services provided by statutory, voluntary or independent organisations.

Substitute decisions

The process, legal or otherwise, by which decisions are made on behalf of someone who is deemed 'mentally incapable' of making decisions for themselves.

Who Decides?

The name of the consultation paper produced by the Lord Chancellor's Department, subtitled 'making decisions on behalf of adults who lack capacity' (1997).

Appendix F
References and resources

Bewley, C (1997) *Money matters: helping people with learning difficulties have more control over their money.* London, VIA.

Bewley, C (1998) *Choice and control: decision-making and people with learning difficulties.* London, VIA.

Canadian Association for Community Living (1998) *Information package on supported decision-making as a rights based alternative to guardianship.* Self Determination and Related Workshops for the XII World congress of Inclusion International. Toronto, Canadian Association for Community Living.

Collins, J (1996) *What's choice got to do with it? A study of housing and support for people with learning difficulties.* London, VIA.

Cooper, J (ed) (2000) *Law, rights and disability.* London, Jessica Kingsley Publishers.

Department of Heath (1990) *Community care in the next decade and beyond: policy guidance.* London, HMSO.

Department of Health (1999) *An easy guide to direct payments.* London, DoH.

Department of Health (2000) *Community Care (Direct Payments) Act 1996: policy and practice guidance*. London, HMSO.

Edge, J and Presley, F (1998) *From isolation to inclusion.* London, Citizen Advocacy Information and Training (CAIT).

Gilbert (1995) in Todd and Gilbert (1995) *Learning disabilities: practice issues in health settings.* London, Routledge.

Golding, W (1959) *Free fall.* London, Faber and Faber.

Henderson, E and Bewley, C (2000) *Too little, too slowly: report on direct payments for people with learning difficulties in Scotland*. London, VIA.

Holman, A (1995) *Independent living for people with learning difficulties: Sample Trust Deed.* London, VIA.

Holman, with Bewley (1999) *Funding freedom 2000: people with learning difficulties using direct payments*. London, VIA.

House of Lords (1997-1998) *Opinions of the Lords of Appeal for judgement in the case of Re L (by his next friend GE) (Respondent)*. Publication on the Internet Session 1997-98.

Jackson, E and Jackson, N (1999) *Helping people with a learning disability explore choice.* London, Jessica Kingsley Publishers.

Keywood, Fovargue and Flynn (1999) **Best Practice? Healthcare decision-making by, with and for adults with learning disabilities.** Manchester, NDT.

Kinsella, P (1993) *Group homes: an ordinary life?* Manchester, National Development Team.

Law Commission (1995) **Report 231, Mental Incapacity,** London, HMSO.

Law Society and British Medical Association (1995) *Assessment of mental capacity: guidance for doctors and lawyers.* London, BMA.

Lord Chancellor's Department (1997) *Who Decides? Making decisions on behalf of mentally incapacitated adults.* London, HMSO.

Lord Chancellor's Department (1999) *Making Decisions: the government's proposals for making decisions on behalf of mentally incapacitated adults.* London, HMSO.

Mandelstam, M (1998) *An A-Z of Community Care Law.* London, Jessica Kingsley Publishers.

Morris, J (1993) *Independent lives? Disabled people and community care.* Basingstoke, Longmans.

Perkins and Repper (1998) *Dilemmas in community mental health practice: choice or control.* Oxon, Radcliffe Medical Press.

Ryan, T. and Holman, A (1998). *Pointers to Control: people with learning difficulties using direct payments*. London, VIA.

Sanderson H, Kennedy J, Ritchie P, & Goodwin G (1997) *People, plans and possibilities.* Edinburgh, Scottish Human Services.

Simons K (1995) *My home, my life.* London, VIA.

Walsh B (1994) *How to set up trusts and user controlled independent living.* London, Independent Living Network of Tower Hamlets.

Wertheimer, A (1998) *Citizen advocacy: a powerful partnership.* London, Citizen Advocacy Information and Training (CAIT).

Williams, P (ed) (1998) *Standing by me: stories of citizen advocacy.* London, Citizen Advocacy Information and Training (CAIT).

Who's in Control?